Cacophony to Calm

Stuti Punshi

BookLeaf
Publishing

India | USA | UK

Presentation by *BookLeaf Publishing*

Web: www.bookleafpub.com

E-mail: info@bookleafpub.com

ISBN: 9789358733617

First edition 2024

DEDICATION

*To my sister; Shreya, a friend, an inspiration, a
guide and a beacon,*

To my parents, my blessing, my joy, my support

*To my everything; Bhaumik; the calm to every
storm, my home.*

ACKNOWLEDGEMENT

Every word that I have written, every rhyme, every creative interlude that I have created, has helped my muddled mind clarify some of its confusing thoughts. The noise around me has always found calm and serenity in ink and paper. This collection is a reflection of those struggles, battles and the eventual triumph of my mind over the turmoil. Writing comes to me in the most unexpected of places and there are many moments when its depth and vivacity surprises me. I have been writing for almost 2 decades now and many times I was told that I was good enough to be published. My insecure and underconfident mind did not want to believe that such a feat could ever be mine, but thankfully, my supporters turned out to be a lot more tenacious and optimistic than this humble poet. And by the grace and blessing of the almighty, being surrounded by endless strength and encouragement from my family, mentors, teachers and friends I am able to present this body of work to you all..

The first of my immense gratitude goes to my family - my parents and my sister. My parents recognised and fired the flame of my creative pursuits and today stand firm and proud behind me as I nervously venture my first offering to the world. Also, I am so lucky to have a sibling who has been a constant champion of my abilities from the very beginning. Always encouraging and helping me recognise my potential. Her wisdom is also reflected within every creation. Shreya, you push me and you make me better.

Secondly, I want to mention two very special teachers who I had the fortune of meeting quite early in my writing journey. I consider myself blessed to have had their guidance and support during those foundational years. Thank you, Mrs. Nidhi Anthony and Mrs. Benedict. My first brush with creative writing occurred under the prodigious mentorship of these ladies and they helped evolve my thoughts into beautiful poetry. Their dedicated encouragement allowed a shy, introverted, and almost apologetic existence to grow into an empathetic and spirited thinker.

Another tremendous contribution to this body of work came from my dear friend, Sunny. He read every first draft and followed that with adulatory praise, along with deserving and honest critiques. Sunny, you introduced me to this challenge in my life and gave me the courage to take it in hand and leap with faith in my words. This collection would not exist without you.

Furthermore, I would like to add a substantial bit of appreciation for my special person, Bhaumik. You were there through every doubtful day, every tear-filled, frustration-filled moment of my journey and you have shown me so much support and encouragement. You have given me happiness and joy beyond belief. You are the true blessing of my life and every day is better with you in it. Half the poems here would not exist if it weren't for you. You have made me better and you make me proud. Thank you, Bunny.

Lastly, I would like to add; what started as a mere poetry challenge, is now a passion-fueled project of which I am tremendously proud. I am most grateful to BookLeaf Publishing for making a lifelong dream come true. The entire team worked with me for months and guided me through those endless edits, revisions and doubts about my work. I thank their design team that helped me find the perfect cover that enveloped all the feelings I have tried to convey in this book. I am forever indebted to them for their time, efforts, patience, skills and meticulous attention to all my needs.

PREFACE

The very first poem I remember reading and absorbing was a simple one.
It ended with...

"Two roads diverged in a wood, and I—
I took the one less traveled by,
And that has made all the difference."

Life was never the same for me. For the longest time, I had lived in a cacophony of anxious thoughts and choices and fear; my solitude stuck to my breath like the irrevocable debris of failures. And then, I saw my light. I began to write. What started as diary entries, random rants in my journal and essays for school and college, soon morphed into something much more beautiful. Those simple feelings and simpler words became song lyrics, which became lyrical rhymes. Albeit the initial themes, soon, my unsaid desires and thoughts found their way to my pages. With endless flowing black ink on a pristine unruled sheet as my savior, my demons began to fade away. I had found my joy.

I still write almost every week. I still carry with me a vintage fountain pen and a small diary. I still capture every heartwarming as well as heartbreaking moment with words. It's my camera and my poems are my gallery of treasured moments. They help me constantly to steal moments of blissful delight in a day filled with the monotony of pursuit.

This collection here is a product of my journey. My pursuit..
Translating every note of noise and chaos into words; every poem is now a haven for my mind. It brings me peace, tranquility, a feeling of coming home. To me words have always been and will always be, my solace and my calm.

Footsteps

Faint footsteps sound so close,
Barred doors and windows, these gusts blow
hard, forcing them to open.
But not even a shadow stands to greet my
guests,
Shattered glass lies from the vase of my rose,
And my eyes, dry now, don't bother anymore to
check what's broken.

Venom

There's no blood on my hands
Just a few scars of a past gone by
No screams escape my pain anymore
They echo silently in my mind, next to where
the skeletons lie.

Funny how my past won't even know me today,
Too many skins one shed.
And just like a snake lying in wait for a prey
fresh,
My own venom has my conscience, my desires
fed.

Their hisses play over and over
Contorting my rage, like molding clay,

Every memory bitter, still fresh like it's from
yesterday,
My eyes, now vacant stare hopelessly ahead,
Turning to stone, any ray daring to penetrate
through the clouds, gray and thick, my way.

Burdens

The burden of my smile
The burden of unspoken pain
The burden of my dreams
The burden of an existence bane

The burden of my prayers
The burden of my scars, of my red stains
The burden of my heavy heart
The burden of silenced words, plain

The burden of forgotten promises
The burden of still feeling the same
The burden of a past still in present, present
The burden of a spirit, brave, in vain

The burden of seconds, hours, days
The burden of pieces of a soul, that now remain
The burden of endless storms without shores,
The burden of relentless rain

The burden of battles forged daily
The burden of my courage slain
The burden of living
The burden of falling, failing, in vain
The burden of empty hands
The burden of trying again.

Villains

I need more vices in my heart.
Harden these soft gates with bars of steel,
Ravens must fly more across the skies of my
mind,
Let those dark clouds, some sunshine steal.

Those shadows have more secrets hidden away,
Their blacks let no weakness reveal,
Like villains veiled, an eclipse their hidden faces
lay,
Every emotion, every weakness, every
advantage held back to conceal.

I need more silence from the music in my mind,
Let my screams echo more clearly, numbingly,
Listen, far more unhinged and harrowing they
will be,
Like an empty orchestra haunting every
memory, like some spoiled victory,
Marred, I want my soul tarnished, soiled like
Villains vilified, just like the rest of me.

Drowning

Drawing in another shaky breath
I steady my treacherous heart once more,
The traitor would give me away in a beat if it
could,
It's overflowing you see, over edges, busting at
seams, drowning me to my very core.

Here, pain feels normal,
Joy remains a foreign feeling somehow,
Fear is comfortable; hope, a dangerous deceit, he
brings me to my knees
Every breath without hope, my faith gets tested
every day now.

Running through this noise, I run far away from
the dreams of promised peace,
Because if I stop, they'll catch me and hold me
still, relentlessly.
My dreams unfulfilled will demand me to climb,
to try again,
My nightmares will tell me to stop, to quit while
I can, helplessly.

When all I can barely do is, breathe in another
shaky breath,
To steady my tear-stained and cracked soul hurt
again,
When all I can I do is barely pretend to smile for
the world closing in,
While I stretch and tear and break, maddeningly
insane.

Tears of Gold

Trampled with sins of my bronzed heart,
Diamond dust in my sighs.
Such an expensive pain to keep,
With tears of gold in my eyes.

Bleeding rubies even in dreams,
Tiaras and shackles adorn the same,
Sparkling smiles weave enchanting lies,
Melting in the same feigned cold flame.

Paying in silver of my bones,
Grinding, to settle debts overdue,

Reflecting glistening pearl tears over the years,
The setting sun catches them with its dying rays
few,

For glories such unbound,
I sold my moth soul to the flames of hell for
free.
And here, I stand with every desire now mine,
Satan would be proud of me.

Scabs

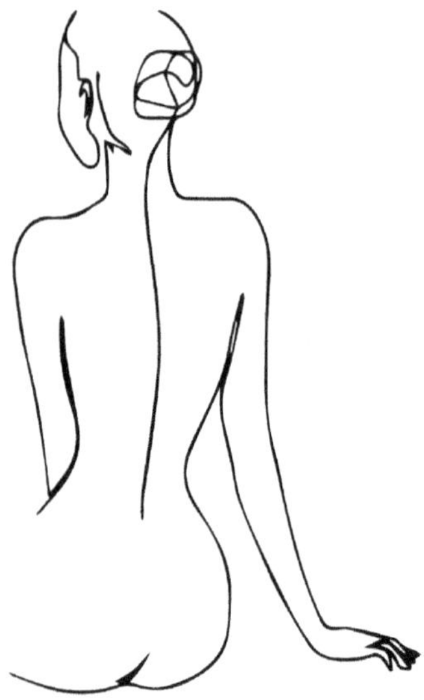

I can't help myself
Picking at these scabs of wounds old
Picking them apart, tearing open my healed skin
I rather bleed thoughts of my yesterdays warm,
than live through these nights cold

So many scars adorn this body
today
A few more would look like old parts of me
Every scar shapes a memory long gone
Letting them bleed, I'll live them once again, just
maybe

Pick, pick, prick I hurt each time
But how else will I know, I live to see another
night cold
I'll bleed my past, my present, memories, stories,
dreams left alone
My moon waits to hear my stories old

Late Nights

I can't sleep at night
The darkness is so inviting you see
These shooting stars paint beautiful dreams for
me
They know my secrets, they use them against me

Such tempting memories they weave
Too close to almost reach out, to feel, I can
almost touch them again
And then again the night steals them away from
me

With fleeting lights, brilliant lies, what use can
the truth be
They envelope my heart, promising me a
paradise long gone
What use can the promise of the day be
With siren songs beckoning my lost soul to a
sunken shore
Tell me, what use can light be

Lies

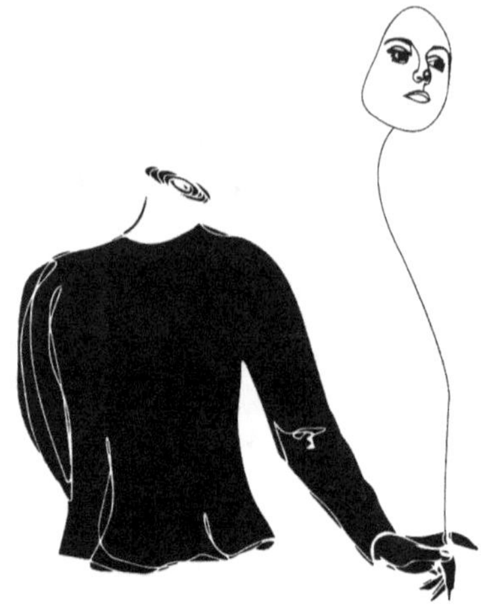

I have learnt to lie too well
With sounds of crashing dreams I'll convince
you too
Say I'm fine with a smile so sweet
Like my heart, I'll fool you too

I have learnt to hide my tears
With pieces of my heart lying shattered before
you
I'll camouflage my face with strength new
And like my gods looking down, I'll sway you
too

I've learnt to pretend too well
With empty hands begging prayers, you'll see
them full of help to you
I'll give my scrapes saying I have enough
Left with nothing again,
The truth, I'll wonder, what good will it do

Conversations with my heart

From the ashes of a burning existence,
With feeble breaths, rise these words like a
phoenix, refusing to die.
Carried by the wind, the crumpled pieces, dust
now, pieces of my heart,
In shards, dormant does every bit lie.

Reveling in its own wake, bruised, so stubbornly
naïve,
It refuses to budge even inches few,
Begging me, teaching me, to breathe, even while
my eyes pool,
It tells me. "We're safe now, for it's just us two."

"Darkness surrounded, alone let us be,
By ourselves, there is no hurt here, there is no
one left to leave,
We won't invite that pesky brain here to join in,
For what purpose will his reasons, causes and
logic achieve".

"Be still my beating heart;" I console, "You have
been used once again,
Don't chase the sun and his fleeting rays,
Learn from your past bleak, know better through
your mistakes disdain,
Know once and for all, like others before him,
he too was never meant to stay."

"Showing you lies in the disguise of dreams,
It's time to let go of vows unmet, it's time to go
away,
This time let's leave before we are left for
another mirage,
Bereft, cursed, alone, in the darkness, again, let
us be on our way."

"Look, how the day teases us, tell that sun to set
his rays a little earlier today,
Could he not blind us anymore, his cheer is
unwelcome to me, reflecting off the dew,

Tell him it hurts, the light, the warmth,
It hurts my eyes, my skin, my wounds, both old
and new."

"Tell him please to let us stay here a little longer,
In shadows we are comfortable, even when we
know it to be a façade true
Because here, I'm not me anymore, I'm not hurt
and you're not broken,
And here, my hands don't stay empty of my
lover's hold too."

The Last Sound

This sound is unlike any other, but
Hearts breaking make beautiful music too.
You make it seem so pleasurably bittersweet my
darling,
Like an art worthy of any canvas, true.

By your hands, I welcome any, every pain,
My love, do what you like to do, this life, this
heart, it is all for you.
For I meant when I vowed, "For better, and for
worse"
When I bound my soul to you.

Even in every piece, made by your words, your hands, I find my peace,
So what, if I'm left with nothing again, left with beats and breaths few,
At least in my absolute ashes I was able to graze a caress new,
By those fingers, enjoy one last touch of you.

Again

Songs, voices, street noises, traffic sounds
mundane,
Any and every sound that I can gather, I play it
over and again.
To fill the silence that envelops me each day
To quiet your memories, my life's woe-filled
bane

They follow me like a shadow, clinging to every
cell of mine
They make me so afraid, always a reminder of
you,
They have taken away my power to be alone,
It was a simpler time, my life before you.

My own mind, a foreign land,
Filled with your songs, voices, words,
memories, all surrounding me,
They threaten to drown me from within,
Just like every lonely place, every silent room
comes to engulf me.

I smile, I talk, I laugh, I listen, I breathe,
Believe me, I walk, I dream, like there never
was, nor will be any trace of you,
But never is there a moment of peace for me,
Because pieces of my heart, though broken and
glued, remember too well, all of you.

I'm daunted by the dark, I'm scared of the
silence too,
Because I know there you'll return to me,
Make me fall in love all over the same,
And just when the flicker of a smile burns my
lips, for sure, once more, you'll leave me.

And recklessly, I'll still reach out and try to hold
on to the figments of a ghost,
A delusion, my own created, I fall prey to tricks
my mind and heart play,
But maybe, if I turn off my lights, my music, my
windows, my doors, my eyes,
This time, you'll choose to stay.

Heart's Hymn

Haunting melancholy perched on those lids
How heavy must be the weight to bear
Forsaken long ago, these abandoned dreams and
hopes
Forgotten, rotten, only their skeleton are now
found here

Among the grays of clouds, dark and overcast
Weighed with relentless thunder and rain
There are glimpses of azures and blue
A lightning spark, seconds long, barely alive,
one hope's due

Lifting those tormented eyes, searching above,
Desolate gaze filled to the brim

A silent screaming plea, begging, urging with
clenched fists
Weeping laments repeating over and over again,
They sound so much like a hymn

With blood-filled veins, bulging through clasped
praying hands
Resolve faint echoes in scars, bruises swollen,
shine too
Etched in every wrinkle is a story of pain
endured
Hope I breathe, knowing even falling stars can
bring wishes true.

What Miracle

What promises can quivering lips speak
What deeds can shaking hands repent
What path can teary eyes seek
Broken souls remain so,
What glue can put together a million pieces,
unimaginably bent

What music can pierce solitude through
What sun, what rays, can cleave apart
Thunderous clouds full of mournful rain,
delicate dew
What miracle l ask every star
Can permeate some light, a halo on the eclipse
of my heart

What repose can still this clamoring noise
What words, what voice can calm my soul's
silent screams

What God watching will soon rejoice
What reality can burn the plight of today, the
nightmare horrid
I wonder what strength I'll gather, assuage which
dream

Borrowed

Borrowed light eclipses so easily
Faithfully this darkness curls next to me
A soft caress every night it bears on my breaking
wounds
Teasing with hope, as I lie here bleeding, so
wantonly

Borrowed smiles fade to die so quickly
Tears I birth, cling to my eyes so unimpeachably,
Unushered, yet never too far away
They'll stain my cheeks, my soul, so shamelessly

Borrowed hello's from strangers known for long
Farewells from them flow so sweetly
Bidding adieu to dreams and promises alike
Mocking my loyalty so beautifully

Borrowed breaths, breathing off my love
My heart hollowed completely

In my solitude, I hear the echo of every beat
Reverberating off those empty walls,
Deafening silence all mine, wrapping me
perfectly.

Still

Her laughter still rings music within me
Her smile unclouded sunshine bright, faint traces
somewhere still buried inside me
Her eyes so dreamy, ablaze with hopes of
tomorrow
Tired now, empty and hopeless they implore me

Little by little I have seen her fire fade away
Die at the very hands of me
I had no choice
Her demise still echoes unspoken horrors for me

Frozen in time her stone heart
Has now forgotten to fight free
My own hands have choked her remnants
Her last breath escaped through me

The knife in her heart, drenched crimson, stains
my hands
Turning from white to red, the very knuckles
gripping the hilt so tightly
I stare at the corpse of the girl l was
Her remains still refusing to die, adamant not to
leave me
Stubborn child, her naïveté fails to understand
How my own hands bestow a blessed mercy
Giving her an out, an exit in time, a death
worthy
Her shine is too golden, that heart too pure,
Too delicate is her shell
The world will not stop hunting, claiming,
stealing, taking
Her soul is too kind, her innocence too precious,
To be piled by the sins of these monsters I see
Yet, her smile still dares to whisper her promise
Her eyes still radiate her love for me

"Let the thunder clouds collect if they must I
welcome all villains and monsters alike to gather
around me
Like broken glass, sharpest in its shards, Like
phoenixes from ashes, like trees bursting from
soil and seeds
Watch them emerge above, behold the rise again
and again,
And darling, so shall we.."

The Last Smile

Filtering through every crack of my glass heart
You marvel at the rainbow mosaic of my pain.
You divert your gaze from the rainbow tears,
That catches the light, brilliantly bright and vain.

My halo bent, my soul crushed,
My wings bloodied, bleeding bright red from
wounds fresh, all over again,
Standing in the ashes of my burnt wishes and
begged prayers,
I smile at my executioner,
My hope scared him insane.

Red

In the wake of corpses all slain dead
The rising sun rays dance, reflecting through all
the blood shed,
I stand alone, my sword drawn and tired, my
armor caked with every drop I bled,
A cathartic scream finally deafens the echoes of
hate,
That noise smiles in the glow of my triumph,
shaded the same yellow, orange and red.

Fire

Fire and flames ablaze with a relentless burn
See her wings, there are no feathers fine and
white
Dare to stare at this hell's angel standing in the
ashes of her soul
Every broken piece of her heart still shines so
bright

Forged like iron, her spirit
Endured trial after trial
Her story, the battles and wars, all are alive in
her eyes
Brought to her knees before, she stands again
Her wings, like a Phoenix, one again shall rise

Embers

Flickering, almost embers faint, blowing away,
A spirit meant to weather through,
A heart beating, searching simply,
For the right beat to beat to.

I see my reflection
I see them seeking another way,
A forlorn soul on its journey, these orbs look up
to me,
Wordlessly, asking for a little more light,
Something, anything from to be.

Wondering, I look again into these eyes of mine
Eyes, crystal, dark, yet kind and true,
They have been hurt, yes, but that flickering
catches my sight,
I want to reach out, save each cinder before it
dies, each one is a hope anew.

So frail, feeble and faint that just a whisper can
be enough douse,
Yet, in colors dark and brown, there is no fearful
hue,
There is only faith, trust, a belief ringing alight,
A desire to simply move along, to happily
continue.

With or without a guiding hand to hold along,
Bright and brave, they turn their bronze gaze
upon me,
Silently promising, that the worst is over,
They tell me to leave it behind where it all
belongs, and I agree.

And as I look back at this mirror,
With resolve new, I stare and see,
A mind altered, a soul converted,
My old smile returns back to me.

Pieces to Peace

I see myself in pieces now
So many pieces, so many parts of me
Scattered, carelessly across the floor,
Broken pieces with broken smiles
Troubled ache, agony sharp, tears within those
shards of me

I see myself in every piece
Parts of my tired soul in every shred, little hurt
bits of me
Yet hear every part still beating,
Rhythms of a broken heart, you see slivers
shining in every piece of me

I see myself in pieces
Reflections in my eyes of a scattered past
But see, how every piece completes me
Every smile, every tear, gluing every pain,
Every joy
Every piece catching the light
All black, all white, those grays mixing in a
rainbow for me

I see myself in pieces darling
Every figment a proud part of me
Holding memories of every struggle, failed,
triumphed stories,
They whisper the audacity of hope, they scream
strength into me
From pieces to peace, I love these pieccs of me.

Armor

Piece by piece, my armor chinks away,
Weary, broken, through brutal battles, fiercely
fought everyday.
And as the sun bears down relentlessly burning
my scarred skin anew,
The rusting metal grows heavy on these
shoulders, tired from wars not few.

Bruised and cracked too far gone, my shields
now threaten to break,
Throat dry and parched to call for help, eyes
weary lie in wake,

Any repair, any respite, any rest seems a mirage
from a past long gone astray,
Tired, breathless, with every step, every mile,
my strength begins to betray.

Yet, to stop now would not be a choice fair,
To give up would be an insult to these bleeding
wounds, bare.
Even with rays unforgiving or rains torrential
beating, my feet will still carry me through
Even with bruised lungs I will draw in shaky
breaths, small but new.

And as seconds of agony turn into hours into
days into a month's rendezvous
Let them turn into tears of years too
Then watch how these lips curve upwards as I
face my maker, above every horizon, yellow and
blue,
Bring it on, I challenge him, watch me burn your
hells, all your wars waged I win, into rubble
your demons I'll breakthrough.

Rainbows

Cry if you must
Each tear is a story you are brave to share
Look how brilliant each drop can be
Even in darkness abound
They make rainbows with the light that you
wear

Woes to words

There's noise deafening in my ears
You wouldn't hear it anywhere near me
Screaming from the anguish of all the hurt
memories replaying in my mind
You wouldn't know to complain with all the
silence around me

My fingers shaking from the fear of being bereft
once again
Maybe that's why you'll always see me holding a
pen, cocooned with words you'll find me
Daggers and knives are an escape kind but
unworthy still
So I choose to write
To rhyme all the chaos within me

Melancholy makes beautiful music I write to
turn to notes, these woes to words inside me

There's darkness bleak, where even shadows
forsake you,
write to break the rays of dawn in this heart of
me
Cloaked I'm clamoring chaos of my world I
write to carry some peace home with me
Overflowing overwhelming thoughts with
tumbling feelings all over
I write to turn into virtuous blessing, all this pain
beholden to me
For all that is lost, for all that is forgotten
I write to keep alive some love inside me I live
in crowds, breathe in cities filled to the brim
I write for the lover in me

I have memories, fine and foe, my moon and
stars, my night and day,
I write for the ghosts of my past, for those who
still walk with me
I write and I smile, knowing I've written well or
even not.
I know I've still poured my heart in ink
I write every beat in words, stories of mine, I
write as I breathe, I write for me...

The girl within me

Her sparkling wide eyes meet mine
Welling to the brim, her gaze searches me
expectantly
Clenched fists open to me, yearning
Lips shaking, tiny mumbles of help, seeking any
shore, she holds on to me so eagerly

Her tears stain my clothes, her cries are begging
me
I look down at her round face, so sweet, so hurt,
scarred so beautifully
Innocent still, her curls just like mine, Brown
like her eyes, like mine,
Darkened with the same pain, she's too young to
bear the weight, the plight she is forced, she
carries it all unwillingly

Crushing under the weight I can hear her
screams she echoes sobbing silently

I know her, I've known her from her first
heartbreak,
So brave was she
I know what broke her and when and how, I
stood by silently
I was witness to every blow, I had no choice but
to bear every moment with her hopelessly

But I have to hold her now, try to calm her
raging sea
Her gentle face, so soft, her tears away I graze
those cheeks carefully So unfamiliar to comfort,
one caress and she falls
Collapses into my arms breaking terribly

I simply smile at her face so adorable, familiar
to me
Her smile could always capture bewitchingly
I hold her, I tell her, I've got you, Your wars are
mine too,
I'll wage them, I'll win them for you I'll teach
you how to survive, guide your delicate heart
through treacherous souls cunningly
A long way still lies ahead of us, And we'll wade
through fearlessly

Every prayer you've made kneeling on the floor
desperately
Your mercy, your savior, your hero is within
you, being honed so admirably
Forgotten, forlorn you may be, but look at what
you've become, nothing breaks you anymore
even vaguely
You still stand tall, proudly I'm you little one,
and you're me Stand and walk and run and rage
and smile through everything thrown your way
adversely
You're stardust, you're sunshine, you're
moonlight, you're raging winds, rainbows bright,
a mosaic of all marvels blended stunningly.

How Many Times?

How many times did you break yourself down?
Into a million pieces, over and over again,
How many times did you let yourself fall and
bleed,
So you could know the taste of your own blood,
bleeding from your veins.

How many times were you brave to say no?
When it was so easy to simply agree,
How many times did you look up to the sky to
pray,
How many star-studded nights did you stay up, a
hope in a shooting star to see?

How many times did the winds, the sun, the
oceans and seas attempt to deter you astray,

Don't you remember how many times you have
fought the tides flowing every wrong way,
Yet, the calm you have earned through every
storm,
Through treacherous tempests you steer to dry
shores and bay.

Tell me my dear, how many times did you repeat
to yourself, how many times did you plead?
Of what verve embodies in every heartbeat, fills
every part of you,
How many times have you strained and
shattered against those chains?
That dared to restrain, constrain, contain the
glory of you.

So remember how many times you have broken
yourself,
See in every piece your renascence over and
over again,
And like molten gold that fills every crack of a
broken crucible or bowl,
Stronger, finer, better, and greater you are made,
from the fortitude of your pain.

His Little Girl

Are you the same little girl?
Who climbed her father's shoulders tall,
Reaching her hands higher and higher each time,
Giggling, feeling like a princess precious,
adored, and loved, who felt she could conquer it
all.

Are you the same little girl,
Who no fear could know, when he stood beside
you, you with your wide eyes, wider smile
shining on that face so small
Dancing and singing with him on his favorites
songs all night
You still remember don't you, the words, the
tunes, the moves to them all?

Are you the same little girl,
Who, he came running to pick up, after each and
every collapse, each and every fall?
He taught you to dust off the bruises with a
smile, or a smirk sly your mother still detests.
Yet, through everything, never faltering, his
strong one, his brave one, his pride and joy, you,
he would call.

I'll tell you, you are the same little girl my dear,
still his princess in his heart,
Your every tear, he cries, your pain hurts him
too, your smile he cherishes like a trophy, your
laughter fills his heart to every brim, overflows
every wall,
Your every memory he carries safe and sound,
stored like mementos of love true, your every
success, your every failure he knows to be his
own,
His hands still hold the impressions of your
hands, tiny that once were there always, he sees
his not so little girl smiling, but still misses those
rides on his shoulders tall.

Cocoon

Straining against every fiber of its making
It's unseemly, ugly, this cocoon I made so tough
and enduring, not easy will it prove to break
through
So lovingly I stitched every thread together, my
haven, my heaven to create here
Now, when it's time to tear it up, my bare hands
will shiver, I will tear apart too

Piece by piece, shredding, shattering, breaking
away
A violent, cathartic, display it will make
My protesting screams, lamenting wails, a
cacophony of chaos and pain
Yet, it's time they all know, the wills of fate, they
can't shake

Pain isn't pretty and blood is red colored
weakness to be left behind
The ashes of my pain, will turn into moldable
clay with the tears I shed
They will water too the seeds of triumph into
roots infallibly deep
Caked with all the torment I bled

So let my wails turn into songs,
My woes sweet poetry shall be
My scars into stories to regale for all
Darling, watch how from the wreckage of my
being, my colored wings, shall spread wide
strong for all to see.

Your Bloom

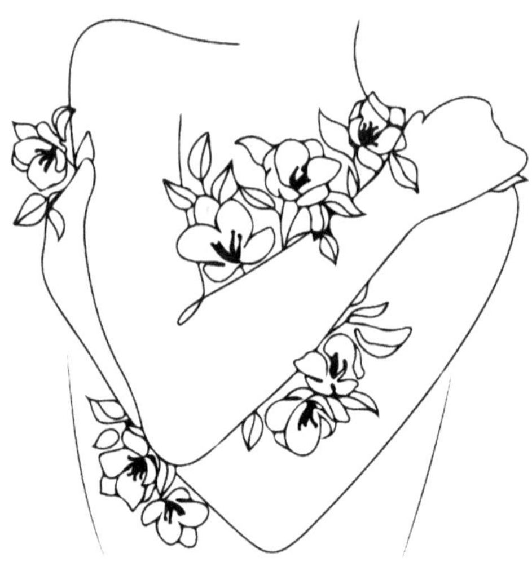

For every ounce of trampled petals from fallen
flowers,
I see spring leaves turning colors, rich,
beautifully green.
For every waning crescent moon approaching a
darker night ahead,
There's the glow of a waxing embrace of a fuller
moon, a glowing dream.

For every roaring thunder up in azure, every
glowering lightning striking brilliantly across the
night sky,
For every storm rumbling under your waters,
menacing your calm,

Look above, and see your sun still shining bright
beyond the clouds,
Your sails still flying high, your oars lie stable,
strong in your palm.

Because you see, eventually even every
caterpillar will learn with its wings new, to break
through, to fly high and away,
Even the darkest dawns will see rays ushering in
a new day,
Even barren trees left desolate in the fall will see
spring, fallen flowers will be reborn, with petals
pretty at display,
Just like that, you too my darling, will bloom
brilliantly, just believe a little more, allow that
faith you hold so dear, to show you your way.

The Wind Speaks

Whispers of the wind caress my aches
Like gentle fingers, soothing my hurt,
Each swaying gush feels like a cleanse deep,
Daring me to smile through it all, like a
shameless flirt.

Every blinking moment brings to me a tranquil
and calm I have not known in a while.
"Why so glum?" the wind dares to ask me.
My vacant eyes answer, brimming with
unushered pain, paired with that pasted smile,

Mere moments from flowing, these tears sit at
the edge of my lids, threatening all my secrets to
spill free.

"Oh dear child, don't you worry a moment more,
I shall dry these little drops of agony even before
you can let them go.
Don't you know how precious are these beads
filled with all your heart, all your love,
Do not let them flow wasted, for others uncaring
or unknown, heartless they are, they don't know.

A heart like yours is beautifully rare,
Mere mortals will always fail searching for a
spirit so kind.
You open your soul to those who are hurt;
remember that brave are such endeavors.
Courage like that remains till date so very hard
to find.

You think your tears make you weak,
You hurt to think that to rest is not okay,
Who taught you that stopping means failing?
That greatness can happen overnight, no pause,
no delay?

Come and sit with me, my child,
We're here for you even if no one else can see,

Every minute, every second, every breath you
draw in to survive,
I see your pain, your bottled cries, your screams
are not silent to me.

Let it all out my dear, I can carry it all far away
from you
You and I came from the same heaven, I know
exactly how and of what stern stuff you were
made.
A force strong, yet with affections so kind,
whose each broken piece shall hold a light bright

Enough to shine every dark corner, always eager
to end the pains, a heart unafraid
Who, even with ashes and scars hurting, bruises
bleeding, will be fair winds in flowing seas,
A full moon in the relentless night,
Under scorching summers, a welcome oasis of
soothing shade."

Calm

I have broken my mirror before,
My reflection blurred, cracked, stays
incomplete, looks back at me,
I see those stains, those streaks of tears,
My own pain, no new stranger to me.

She comes to me every time with a new
disguise,
Cloaked in lessons, rewards and retributions, I
welcome her all,

Hidden in such sweet deceiving disguise,
She tries my resolve, tries to own it, make it
small.

My love, my fire, my journey, my heart, all of
me,
Every scar, glorified, embraced is every crevice,
every line, every wrinkle is cherished for what it
stands to be,
See how my reflection in this old mirror now
smiles back at me,
Oh, she looks so proud in her armor, just as she
should be.

Darkness knew me long, knew me too well,
Today his friend stands before my eyes,
introducing his light to my heart and mind,
And today, happiness knows me by name proud,
Joining in the celebration, all my past cacophony
takes part, my calm smile returns to all in
gratitude, kind.

All debts paid, this light is mine to keep,
To say, be relieved, take a breath, the best is on
its way to you, to stay this time,
All your strength, all your weakness, wrapped in
one face, one body, one soul, one mind,
With the edges still rough from all the climbs,
look how that shield glistens, happy tears shine.

www.ingramcontent.com/pod-product-compliance
Lightning Source LLC
LaVergne TN
LVHW021212200726
843509LV00012B/1431